Christian for One Day

The Man Who Was Beheaded the Day He Became a Christian

Dina M. Jones

DAIV House Publications

Christian for One Day by Dina M. Jones.

©2017 Dina M. Jones. All rights reserved.

No part of this book may be reproduced in any written, electronic, recording, or photocopying without written permission of the publisher or author. The exception would be in the case of brief quotations embodied in the critical articles or reviews and pages where permission is specifically granted by the publisher or author.

Although every precaution has been taken to verify the accuracy of the information contained herein, the author and publisher assume no responsibility for any errors or omissions.

Christian For One Day

Table of Contents

Introduction	1
Chapter 1	3
Chapter 2	9
Chapter 3	12
Chapter 4	18
Chapter 5	26
Chapter 6	30
Acknowledgements	34
BIBLIOGRAPHY	35

Christian For One Day

Introduction

Through their strong faith, the Coptic Christians are showing us how to overcome evil with good.

My book, Beheaded, was named in reference to Revelation Chapter 20 verse 4, which states,

And I saw thrones, and they sat upon them, and judgment was given unto them: and *I saw* the souls of them that were beheaded for the witness of Jesus, and for the word of God, and which had not worshipped the beast, neither his image, neither had received *his* mark upon their foreheads, or in their hands; and they lived and reigned with Christ a thousand years.

Christian For One Day

This refers to the Christians who will be martyred during the reign of the antichrist.

As we see in our lives today, Christians are being beheaded for their beliefs. But during the reign of the antichrist, the tribulation and death of believers in Christ will be astronomical. But there is hope.

Matthew Chapter 24 verse 22 states,

And except those days should be shortened, there should no flesh be saved: but for the elect's sake those days shall be shortened.

Those words were spoken by Jesus Christ when the disciples asked about the events leading to the end of the world. Jesus was referring to the Christians who will be here during the tribulation, not WRATH of God. There is a BIG difference.

This book was written in truth and with humor. The words in italics are verses/ words spoken by Jesus Christ. May God bless you.

Chapter 1

You may have heard of the story of the 21 Coptic Christians from Egypt, who held fast to their faith and were beheaded by ISIS in February, 2015. But did you know that only 20 of them were actually Copts from Egypt? Did you know that one of the martyrs was from Chad, and he had not been a Christian prior to the day of his beheading?

All 21 men had been working in Libya when they were kidnapped by ISIS. One of them had darker skin and different facial features. This can be seen in pictures where they are lined up on the beach to be killed. This was the man from Chad.

Christian For One Day

This reminds me of the parable of the landowner who hired laborers for the day and paid them the same wage, regardless of the hours worked.

Matthew Chapter 20 verses 1-16 states,

"For the kingdom of heaven is like a landowner who went out early in the morning to hire workers for his vineyard. He agreed to pay them a denarius for the day and sent them into his vineyard.

"About nine in the morning he went out and saw others standing in the marketplace doing nothing. He told them, 'You also go and work in my vineyard, and I will pay you whatever is right.' So they went.

"He went out again about noon and about three in the afternoon and did the same thing. About five in the afternoon he went out and found still others standing around. He asked them, 'Why have you been standing here all day long doing nothing?'

"'Because no one has hired us,' they answered.

"He said to them, 'You also go and work in my vineyard.'

Christian For One Day

"When evening came, the owner of the vineyard said to his foreman, 'Call the workers and pay them their wages, beginning with the last ones hired and going on to the first.'

"The workers who were hired about five in the afternoon came and each received a denarius. So when those came who were hired first, they expected to receive more. But each one of them also received a denarius. When they received it, they began to grumble against the landowner. 'These who were hired last worked only one hour,' they said, 'and you have made them equal to us who have borne the burden of the work and the heat of the day.'

"But he answered one of them, 'I am not being unfair to you, friend. Didn't you agree to work for a denarius? Take your pay and go. I want to give the one who was hired last the same as I gave you. Don't I have the right to do what I want with my own money? Or are you envious because I am generous?'

"So the last will be first, and the first will be last."

Christian For One Day

Let me restate what you have just read. This parable teaches that it doesn't matter to God when He calls you as a believer. Unfortunately, some Christians who have been believers for a long time think they deserve more than newer Christians. I was also guilty of this in the past.

In the parable, the workers who had been working all day felt they should be paid more and found it an insult to receive the same amount of money as the workers who were there for only an hour.

The landowner (metaphor for God) told them, you agreed to work for a denarius (about $100 in today's money) and this man agreed to work for the same amount. (You agreed to accept salvation and this man agreed to accept salvation). You were paid what you agreed to no matter how long you have been here. Plus, this is my land and I make the rules. (He is God; He can do whatever He wants to do)!

When we agree to become believers in Christ, we are all the same in His eyes, whether it was 60 years ago or today. We all receive the same reward, which is salvation! Eternal life!

The man from Chad, although he became a believer just one day before his death, earned the right to live in heaven with the other Coptic Christians, forever. Amen!

Additionally, the Gospel of Luke describes two thieves, being on either side of Jesus as they were crucified. At that very point of death by Crucifixion, one of the thieves accepted Christ.

Luke 23 verses 39-43 states,

One of the criminals who hung there hurled insults at him: "Aren't you the Messiah? Save yourself and us!"

But the other criminal rebuked him. "Don't you fear God," he said, "since you are under the same sentence? We are punished justly, for we are getting what our deeds deserve. But this man has done nothing wrong."

Then he said, "Jesus, remember me when you come into your kingdom."

Jesus answered him, "Truly I tell you, today you will be with me in paradise."

Christian For One Day

To God, it's not the matter of time spent as a Christian, it's the matter of faith.

Chapter 2

The Coptic Christians were given a choice to deny Jesus or die. They refused to deny Him, knowing it would cost them their heads. When the terrorists ordered the man from Chad to deny Jesus or die, he answered, "Their God is my God," thereby sealing his fate.

Luke 12 verses 8-9 states,

"I tell you, whoever publicly acknowledges me before others, the Son of Man will also acknowledge before the angels of God. But whoever disowns me before others will be disowned before the angels of God."

During the reign of the antichrist, Christians will be given the choice to worship

Christian For One Day

the antichrist, his image, receive his mark or his number, 666. Either you will publicly confess your allegiance to the antichrist or you will publicly confess your allegiance to Jesus.

Years ago, when I was a self-conscious teenager, overly concerned about public embarrassment, I was riding the bus. I was sitting near the front. The bus stopped and picked up this girl who was in her early 20s. She came onto the quiet bus, smiling at everyone, then took a seat near me. In a not-so-conversational voice, she asked me, "Do you know Jesus?" I was mortified.

Everyone turned and looked right at me. I felt the eyes glaring at me, waiting for my response. I have to admit, I can't remember if I knew the verses from Luke 12 or not. But as I pondered what to say, paralyzed with fear, the fear suddenly went away, as I boldly AND publicly said; Yes, yes I know Jesus. I felt a sense of peace come over me as she said, "That's good, good for you."

What I can tell you is that upon learning this verse and remembering this incident, I

Christian For One Day

thought, Jesus, that's what I did, publicly declared my faith in You! Hallelujah!

Now of course, there is no comparison of these Coptic Christians and the man from Chad. They were staring death in the face. I was just a self-conscious young girl staring fear in the face. But the similarity is to publicly declare knowing Jesus.

Chapter 3

The man from Chad was so moved by the faith of those Christians. Their refusal to deny their Savior, even at the point of death — literally, at the point of a knife to their throats — which by the way, this was no typical beheading. No guillotine. No ax. It has been described that their heads were CARVED from their bodies. I saw the images. Absolutely horrific. Yet, despite this imminent fate, he had the strength to make a profession of faith, publicly, one that would cost him his head and of course, his life.

Can we grasp the intensity of this story? How many Christians would be tempted to save their life under such circumstances?

How many would waver and, for that moment, deny their Lord, just to avoid beheading? Yet this man, who had not been a follower of Jesus before then, was so moved by the dedication of these Christians that he became a believer on the spot.

"Go ahead and behead me," he was saying. "Your god is not my God. Their God is my God."

This demonstration of true faith is the reason, I believe, some Christians, during the tribulation, will be beheaded. (If you believe Christians will not be here during the tribulation, sometimes called the pre-tribulation rapture, they will. Tribulation is not the WRATH of God. For an explicit explanation of this and other controversial topics in the book of Revelation, read my book, Beheaded)!

When faced with the life or death choice of accepting the antichrist and live (yet, going to hell) or continue to follow Jesus and die.

John Chapter 11 verses 25-26 states,

Jesus said, "I am the resurrection and the life. The one who believes in me will live, even though they die; and whoever lives by believing in me will never die."

Some Christians, are Laodicean-type Christians. In the book of Revelation, these were Christians that Jesus had John write a letter. Jesus was upset with them because they had a religion of boasting words, but devoid of vitality and moral strength.

In other words, they were neither hot nor cold for Jesus, they were lukewarm. Jesus metaphorically, spit them from His mouth due to their lack of commitment either way.

Think of it as a cup of coffee. Most people like it cold. Some people like it hot. Almost all find it unpleasant **lukewarm.**

But in that moment of truth, with the knife at your throat, you will be either hot for Jesus and be willing to die like these men or cold towards Him, just to "save" your life. Save is in quotations because at that point in time, although you will save your human life, you will lose your soul, your eternal life.

Eternity is a long time compared to this whisper of time we call life.

Christian For One Day

Jesus said in Luke Chapter 9 verses 23-26,

Then he said to them all: "Whoever wants to be my disciple must deny themselves and take up their cross daily and follow me. For whoever wants to save their life will lose it, but whoever loses their life for me will save it. What good is it for someone to gain the whole world, and yet lose or forfeit their very self? Whoever is ashamed of me and my words, the Son of Man will be ashamed of them when he comes in his glory and in the glory of the Father and of the holy angels."

Additionally, I see this as a repeat of history. The disciples said they would never deny Jesus.

Matthew Chapter 26 verses 34-35 states,

"Truly I tell you," Jesus answered, "this very night, before the rooster crows, you will disown me three times."

But Peter declared, "Even if I have to die with you, I will never disown you." And all the other disciples said the same.

After Jesus had been arrested, Peter witnessed the trial. When the time came for

Christian For One Day

Peter to admit knowing Jesus, this was what happened.

Matthew Chapter 26 verses 69-74 states,

Now Peter was sitting out in the courtyard, and a servant girl came to him. "You also were with Jesus of Galilee," she said.

But he denied it before them all. "I don't know what you're talking about," he said.

Then he went out to the gateway, where another servant girl saw him and said to the people there, "This fellow was with Jesus of Nazareth."

He denied it again, with an oath: "I don't know the man!"

After a little while, those standing there went up to Peter and said, "Surely you are one of them; your accent gives you away."

Then he began to call down curses, and he swore to them, "I don't know the man!"

Immediately a rooster crowed. Then Peter remembered the word Jesus had spoken: "Before the rooster crows, you will disown me three times." And he went outside and wept bitterly.

Christian For One Day

This will not work during the reign of the antichrist. If you deny Jesus, that means you are siding with the devil and you will be FORCED to worship him and take his mark. When you do that, you will be damned, AUTOMATICALLY for eternity! There is no forgiveness, no turning back. Do not collect $200 dollars, go straight to hell! (Monopoly game metaphor, sorry).

In the end, Jesus forgave the disciples upon His resurrection. They are guaranteed that their names will be placed on the wall of the New Jerusalem.

Revelation Chapter 21 verse 14 states,

And the wall of the city had twelve foundations, and in them the names of the twelve apostles of the Lamb.

Deny Jesus and worship the antichrist, your name will not be found anywhere. Most importantly, instead of your name being written, it will be blotted OUT of the book of life.

Chapter 4

The man from Chad had not been a believer. All he had to say was, "I don't believe in Jesus" or, "Jesus is not the Son of God," and he could walk away a free man. He would be with his family again. He would not die a brutal death. He would live to see another day.

But Jesus said in John Chapter 12 verses 25-26,

He that loveth his life shall lose it; and he that hateth his life in this world shall keep it unto life eternal.

If any man serve me, let him follow me; and where I am, there shall also my servant be: if any man serve me, him will my Father honour.

The disciples, when the Roman persecutors came to arrest Jesus, ran away so they would not be prosecuted and put to death. They chose to save their lives instead of being crucified along with Him.

Albeit, I'm pretty sure, from what we know medically, crucifixion is extremely long and painful. This would scare anyone! Comparing that to the swift death by beheading, and given the option, beheading would be a better choice.

But as Jesus states in Luke Chapter 12 verses 4-5,

"I tell you, my friends, do not be afraid of those who kill the body and after that can do no more. But I will show you whom you should fear: Fear him who, after your body has been killed, has authority to throw you into hell. Yes, I tell you, fear him."

That is how we overcome Satan, by not loving our lives when faced with death.

Christian For One Day

Revelation Chapter 12 verse 11 states,

And they overcame him by the blood of the Lamb, and by the word of their testimony; and they loved not their lives unto the death.

In other words, be willing to stand up for your belief in Christ and die for Him.

There is a tag line associated with my book, Beheaded. It says, Do you want to live forever? Then, get Beheaded. It's a double entendre or has double meaning. You can read my book, Beheaded, and learn through the simple explanation of the book of Revelation how to save your life (soul) OR when the time comes to profess your allegiance, to the devil or Christ, choose being beheaded to spend eternity in heaven.

That is why this story needs to be told and retold until the faith of those martyrs becomes our faith, until people look at our lives and say, "Your God is my God, whatever may come my way."

Believers faced with death, but overcoming and ultimately proving their God is the one true God to non-believing persecutors, is a story told many times in the Bible.

One example is in the book of Daniel Chapter 3 verses 19-29 which states,

Then Nebuchadnezzar was furious with Shadrach, Meshach and Abednego, and his attitude toward them changed. He ordered the furnace heated seven times hotter than usual and commanded some of the strongest soldiers in his army to tie up Shadrach, Meshach and Abednego and throw them into the blazing furnace. So, these men, wearing their robes, trousers, turbans and other clothes, were bound and thrown into the blazing furnace.

The king's command was so urgent and the furnace so hot that the flames of the fire killed the soldiers who took up Shadrach, Meshach and Abednego, and these three men, firmly tied, fell into the blazing furnace.

Then King Nebuchadnezzar leaped to his feet in amazement and asked his advisers, "Weren't there three men that we tied up and threw into the fire?"

They replied, "Certainly, Your Majesty."

He said, "Look! I see four men walking around in the fire, unbound and unharmed, and the fourth looks like a son of the gods."

Nebuchadnezzar then approached the opening of the blazing furnace and shouted, "Shadrach, Meshach and Abednego, servants of the Most High God, come out! Come here!"

So, Shadrach, Meshach and Abednego came out of the fire, and the satraps, prefects, governors and royal advisers crowded around them. They saw that the fire had not harmed their bodies, nor was a hair of their heads singed; their robes were not scorched, and there was no smell of fire on them.

Then Nebuchadnezzar said, "Praise be to the God of Shadrach, Meshach and Abednego, who has sent his angel and rescued his servants! They trusted in him and defied the king's command and were willing to give up their lives rather than serve or worship any god except their own God. Therefore, I decree that the people of any nation or language who say anything against the God of Shadrach, Meshach and Abednego be cut into pieces and their houses be turned into piles of rubble, for no other god can save in this way."

Another example is the story of King Darius and Daniel being thrown into the lions' den.

Daniel Chapter 6 verses 15-27 states,

Then the men went as a group to King Darius and said to him, "Remember, Your Majesty, that according to the law of the Medes and Persians no decree or edict that the king issues can be changed."

So the king gave the order, and they brought Daniel and threw him into the lions' den. The king said to Daniel, "May your God, whom you serve continually, rescue you!"

A stone was brought and placed over the mouth of the den, and the king sealed it with his own signet ring and with the rings of his nobles, so that Daniel's situation might not be changed. Then the king returned to his palace and spent the night without eating and without any entertainment being brought to him. And he could not sleep.

At the first light of dawn, the king got up and hurried to the lions' den. When he came near the den, he called to Daniel in an anguished voice, "Daniel, servant of the living God, has your God, whom you serve continually, been able to rescue you from the lions?"

Daniel answered, "May the king live forever! My God sent his angel, and he shut the mouths of the lions. They have not hurt me, because I was found innocent in his sight. Nor have I ever done any wrong before you, Your Majesty."

The king was overjoyed and gave orders to lift Daniel out of the den. And when Daniel was lifted from the den, no wound was found on him, because he had trusted in his God.

At the king's command, the men who had falsely accused Daniel were brought in and thrown into the lions' den, along with their wives and children. And before they reached the floor of the den, the lions overpowered them and crushed all their bones.

Then King Darius wrote to all the nations and peoples of every language in all the earth:

"May you prosper greatly!

Christian For One Day

"I issue a decree that in every part of my kingdom people must fear and reverence the God of Daniel.

"For he is the living God and he endures forever; his kingdom will not be destroyed, his dominion will never end. He rescues and he saves; he performs signs and wonders in the heavens and on the earth. He has rescued Daniel from the power of the lions."

These are just a few examples of how the faith, of a believer in God, changed a nonbeliever into a believer. Amen!

Chapter 5

There are many stories of Christians being martyred in today's society. At the World Summit in Defense of Persecuted Christians, the daughter of an Iranian pastor, martyred 20 years ago, spoke of her own life experience and of her father's refusal to back down. Now, 20 years after her father was buried in an unmarked grave, she could speak of multiplied hundreds of thousands of Iranian Muslims coming to faith in Jesus. Her father's blood was not shed in vain.

Jesus told His disciples as He predicted His own death.

Christian For One Day

John Chapter 12 verses 24-25 states,

"Very truly I tell you, unless a kernel of wheat falls to the ground and dies, it remains only a single seed. But if it dies, it produces many seeds."

The death of this Iranian pastor produced many "seeds." (Believers in Jesus).

A Syrian Christian leader shared how a radical Islamic group offered to arm them (give them weapons) to fight against another radical Islamic faction. He replied, "We already have two arms, love and forgiveness. We don't want to become another militia."

I love his use of the word "arm". While they meant weapons, the Christian leader meant human arms. Wow.

When being persecuted, how many times do you forgive your enemy? Peter asked Jesus this very question.

Matthew Chapter 18 verses 21-22 states,

Then came Peter to him, and said, Lord, how oft shall my brother sin against me, and I forgive him? Till seven times?

Christian For One Day

Jesus saith unto him, *I say not unto thee, Until seven times: but, Until seventy times seven.*

That is how you overcome evil with good. I know it's hard, very hard, but I have practiced this in my own life. And I am at peace in my body, mind, and soul.

It would be wrong to think of these suffering believers as super saints, which is another lesson for us to learn.

Most of them are just ordinary Christians, not preachers or pastors, and certainly not big-name evangelists. They are mothers and fathers, young people and old people, laborers and housewives, educated and uneducated.

Yet, they have remained faithful under hellish pressure, enduring unspeakable suffering. Rather than curse God, they bless Him, and rather than retaliate against their enemies with hatred and vengeance, they offer forgiveness and love.

Romans Chapter 12 verses 14-21 states,

Bless those who persecute you; bless and do not curse. Rejoice with those who rejoice;

mourn with those who mourn. Live in harmony with one another. Do not be proud, but be willing to associate with people of low position. Do not be conceited.

Do not repay anyone evil for evil. Be careful to do what is right in the eyes of everyone. If it is possible, as far as it depends on you, live at peace with everyone. Do not take revenge, my dear friends, but leave room for God's wrath, for it is written: "It is mine to avenge; I will repay," says the Lord. On the contrary:

"If your enemy is hungry, feed him; if he is thirsty, give him something to drink. In doing this, you will heap burning coals on his head."

Do not be overcome by evil, but overcome evil with good.

Moreover, I will add, do this as HUMANLY as possible. The Bible states, for there is none righteous, no, not one. We strive to be like Jesus although we are mere mortals who are not perfect. This is not an excuse, but a reality.

Chapter 6

Earlier this year, a couple told the story about their trip to Ethiopia where they met with family members of the Ethiopian Christians beheaded by ISIS. They spoke with the widow of one of the martyrs who was pregnant when he was killed, making his death even more painful.

But when they talked with this young woman, rather than bemoan her terrible loss, she said to them, "How is it that I had the privilege of being married to a martyr for Jesus?" She had no formal education. No social status. And she was humbled beyond words that she was chosen to be the wife of a martyr.

Christian For One Day

This is why we should stop feeling sorry for ourselves when things get a little rough.

Romans Chapter 8 verses 31-39

If God is for us, who can be against us? He who did not spare his own Son, but gave him up for us all—how will he not also, along with him, graciously give us all things? Who will bring any charge against those whom God has chosen? It is God who justifies. Who then is the one who condemns? No one. Christ Jesus who died—more than that, who was raised to life—is at the right hand of God and is also interceding for us. Who shall separate us from the love of Christ? Shall trouble or hardship or persecution or famine or nakedness or danger or sword? As it is written:

"For your sake we face death all day long; we are considered as sheep to be slaughtered. " No, in all these things we are more than conquerors through him who loved us. For I am convinced that neither death nor life, neither angels nor demons, neither the present nor the future, nor any powers, neither height nor depth, nor anything else in all creation, will be able to separate us from the love of God that is in Christ Jesus our Lord. Hallelujah!

Ultimately, every evil will fall before the name of Jesus.

Romans Chapter 14 verse 11 states,

It is written: "As surely as I live,' says the Lord, '**every knee** will **bow** before me; **every** tongue will confess that Jesus Christ is Lord."

Additionally, this is why every other force that seeks to wipe out believers will fail in the end.

Romans Chapter 8 verses 28-30 states,

And we know that in all things God works for the good of those who love him, who have been called according to his purpose. For those God foreknew he also predestined to be conformed to the image of his Son, that he might be the firstborn among many brothers and sisters. And those he predestined, he also called, those he called, he also justified; those he justified, he also glorified.

Christian For One Day

From this moment forward, remember the faith, shining through those 20 Christians, who made a non-believer, become a true believer in Christ, even at the point of death.

Whether you are staring death in the face or when you are going through the storms of life.

Remember Philippians Chapter 4 verse 13 states,

I can do all things through Christ which strengthens me.

May God help all of us to strengthen our faith, so that the world may see our good works, and glorify our Father which is in heaven. (Taken from Matthew Chapter 5 verse 16).

If you want to live forever, Get Beheaded today. (The book, of course!) Amen.

Acknowledgements

I would like to thank the following:

God the Father, Jesus Christ, and the Holy Spirit.

My children for their support, love and inspiration.

For everyone else who inspired, contributed, and supported this book.

I love you all, thank you.

BIBLIOGRAPHY

Original article from Ask Dr. Brown Ministries. Used with permission.

Bible verses are from the KJV bible:

The Holy Bible, King James Version. Cambridge Edition: 1769; *King James Bible Online,* 2017. www.kingjamesbibleonline.org.

Bible verses are from the NIV bible:

NIV bible. Used with permission. All rights reserved.